count on us...™

cookbook of new and delicious recipes

MARKS &
SPENCER

Marks and Spencer p.l.c.

Baker Street, London W1U 8EP

www.marksandspencer.com

Created and produced by The Bridgewater Book Company Ltd.

Marks and Spencer would like to thank Fiona Hunter
The count on us... cookbook was written in association with Fiona Hunter, a qualified nutritionist
and dietician. Fiona has over 20 years' experience in the field of nutrition, including seven years
working for the National Health Service. She now writes regularly for a number of magazines
and newspapers. Women's health issues and the problems of obesity are areas
of particular interest to Fiona.

Marks and Spencer would also like to thank Karen Thomas (photographer), Valerie Berry (home economist),
Breda Bradshaw (home economist) and Charlie Parker (marketing nutritionist).

ISBN: 1-84273-897-6

Printed in China

NOTES

This symbol means the recipe is suitable for vegetarians.

This book uses both metric and imperial measurements. Follow the same
units of measurement throughout; do not mix metric and imperial.

All spoon measurements are level unless otherwise specified.

Recipes using raw or very lightly cooked eggs should be avoided by infants, the elderly,
pregnant women, convalescents, and anyone suffering from an illness.

The times given are an approximate guide only. Preparation times differ according
to the techniques used by different people and the cooking times may also vary from those given.
Optional ingredients, variations or serving suggestions have not been included in the calculations.

DISCLAIMER

*Before following any of the advice given in this book we recommend that you first check with your doctor.
Pregnant women, women planning to become pregnant, children, diabetics or people with other medical
conditions should always check with their doctor or health care professional before embarking on any type
of diet. This book is not intended as a substitute for your doctor's or dietician's advice and support, but
should complement the advice they give you. The accuracy of the nutritional information (calorie, fat and
salt) given for each recipe is dependent on following the recipe instructions.*

CONTENTS

introduction

HOW TO USE YOUR COUNT ON US... COOKBOOK

Losing weight isn't always easy, but the benefits are enormous – you'll feel fitter and more confident, you'll have more energy and you'll be healthier. The good news is that losing weight doesn't mean having to say goodbye to your favourite foods, in fact it's important to include the foods you enjoy eating. A diet which leaves you feeling deprived, unhappy and dissatisfied is a diet that's very quickly going to be abandoned.

With increasing pressure on our daily schedule many of us don't always have the time to cook meals from scratch, which is why Marks and Spencer have developed the **count on us...** range. **count on us...** has been developed for people who love their food but want to lose a little weight. All the products in the range are less than 3% fat, calorie-controlled and low in salt.

The range has been designed to provide a nutritionally balanced eating plan for women with a target intake of around 1400 calories a day and for men of around 2000 calories a day. The aim is to help people achieve gradual but steady and sustained weight loss.

Breakfast   Lunch

Main meal   Dessert

There are over 150 products in the range, from breakfasts and snacks to quick lunches and main meals. Following a diet can be very boring if you have to eat the same foods day after day so we're continually developing new products to include favourite dishes, which would normally be forbidden in most diets.

The recipes in this book are intended to complement the **count on us...** range; each recipe comes with a nutritional breakdown of the calorie, total fat, saturated fat and salt content.

HEALTHY EATING
A BALANCED APPROACH TO HEALTHY EATING

The food we eat can have an important and lasting effect on our health. Our body needs over 40 different nutrients to stay healthy. Some, such as carbohydrates, proteins and fats, are required in relatively large quantities, while others, such as vitamins, minerals and trace elements, are required in minute amounts but are no less essential for health.

> *The best way to ensure that we get the full range of all the nutrients our bodies need is to eat a varied diet containing foods from each of the 5 food groups.*
> *The secret to healthy eating and managing your weight is to get the balance right.*

BALANCE OF GOOD HEALTH

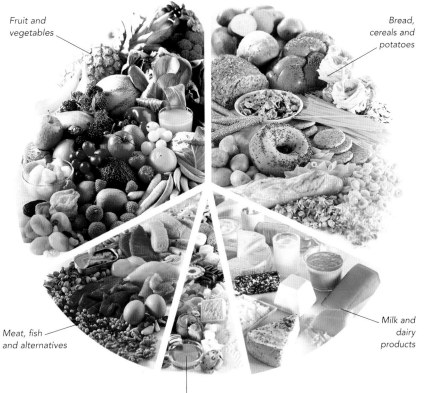

Fruit and vegetables

Bread, cereals and potatoes

Meat, fish and alternatives

Foods containing fats and/or sugar

Milk and dairy products

Based on the Balance of Good Health with kind permission of the Food Standards Agency

BREAD, CEREALS AND POTATOES (E.G. BREAD, RICE, PASTA, NOODLES, BREAKFAST CEREALS) – KNOWN AS COMPLEX OR STARCHY CARBOHYDRATES

Foods from this group should provide around one-third of your calories each day. These foods provide carbohydrates, dietary fibre, protein, vitamins and minerals but their main job is to provide energy.

Choose fibre-rich varieties such as wholemeal bread and wholegrain cereals – they provide slow-release energy which helps keep blood sugar levels stable.

Contrary to what many people believe, foods from this group are not fattening in themselves, becoming highly calorific only when eaten with lots of fat (a rich, creamy sauce with pasta, fried potatoes, or bread spread thickly with butter).

• Depending on your appetite and calorie requirement aim to eat between
  6 and 11 servings from this group each day.

1 serving equals:
3tbsp breakfast cereal
1 slice bread
2 heaped tbsp boiled rice
3 heaped tbsp pasta
2 egg-sized potatoes

FRUIT AND VEGETABLES

It's no coincidence that people from Mediterranean countries who eat almost twice the amount of fruit and vegetables we do live longer and remain healthier. Fruit and vegetables provide vitamins and minerals, dietary fibre and phytochemicals, which may help protect against diseases such as cancer and heart disease.

The advice from experts is that we should all aim to eat at least 5 portions of fruit and vegetables a day. This has been proved to help prevent a number of diseases including heart disease and several forms of cancer.

Apart from being excellent providers of vitamins and minerals, most fruit and vegetables are fat-free and wonderfully low in calories. Make the most of them and look out for new recipes and ideas for cooking them – try poaching, baking or grilling fruits as an alternative to eating them raw.

- Aim to eat at least 5 portions of fruit and vegetables a day.
- Adopt a rainbow approach – different coloured fruit and vegetables provide different vitamins and minerals.
- Frozen, canned and dried fruits and vegetables as well as juices are all useful in helping you reach your daily target.

1 serving equals 80g (3oz) of fruit or vegetables, a total of 400g (14oz) per day:

Fresh

Frozen

Dried

Canned

1 small glass (150ml/5fl oz) unsweetened fruit juice

1 slice melon or pineapple

1 apple, orange, peach or pear

80g (3oz) frozen peas, sweetcorn or berries

1 x 15ml sp (1tbsp) dried fruit e.g. raisins

3 x 15ml sp (3tbsp) fruit salad or canned fruit or vegetables

MILK AND DAIRY PRODUCTS (E.G. MILK, YOGHURT, CHEESE) – THIS GROUP DOES NOT INCLUDE BUTTER, EGGS AND CREAM

Dairy products are an important source of calcium, essential for strong bones and teeth. Many people, especially teenage girls, fail to eat enough calcium to meet their recommended daily requirement – putting them at risk of the bone disease osteoporosis in later life. As many as 1 in 3 women and 1 in 12 men over the age of 50 in the UK suffer from osteoporosis.

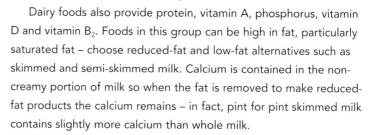

Dairy foods also provide protein, vitamin A, phosphorus, vitamin D and vitamin B_2. Foods in this group can be high in fat, particularly saturated fat – choose reduced-fat and low-fat alternatives such as skimmed and semi-skimmed milk. Calcium is contained in the non-creamy portion of milk so when the fat is removed to make reduced-fat products the calcium remains – in fact, pint for pint skimmed milk contains slightly more calcium than whole milk.

- Aim to eat between 2 and 3 servings from this group a day.
- Choose low- and reduced-fat varieties whenever possible.

1 serving equals:
1 glass milk (200ml/⅓pint)
150g (5oz) yoghurt
100g (3½oz) cottage cheese
40g (1½oz) hard full-fat cheese e.g. Cheddar

MEAT, FISH AND ALTERNATIVES
(POULTRY, EGGS, BEANS AND PULSES, NUTS AND SEEDS)

Foods from this group provide protein, needed for the production of enzymes, antibodies and hormones – in short, protein is vital to ensure our bodies function properly. In the UK, we commonly have plenty of protein in our diet. Foods in this group are also a good source of iron, needed by the blood to circulate oxygen around the body. As many as 1 in 3 women in the UK have been found to have low iron stores, which causes tiredness, lethargy and possibly anaemia.

• Aim to eat between 2 and 4 servings from this group a day.
• Meat should be lean with any visible fat removed before cooking.
• Meat can be fresh, frozen or part of a prepared meal.
• Aim to eat 1–2 servings of oil-rich fish such as salmon, mackerel or tuna a week. All are rich in omega-3 fatty acids, and help to reduce the risk of heart disease.
• Vegetarians should eat a variety of different protein foods to ensure they get all the nutrients they need.

1 serving equals approximately:
90g (3½oz) red meat
125g (4oz) chicken
125–150g (4–5oz) fish
5tbsp baked beans
2tbsp nuts

FOODS CONTAINING FATS AND SUGARS

Small amounts of fat are vital in our diet to provide essential fatty acids and to facilitate the absorption of fat-soluble vitamins, but a high-fat diet is known to increase the risk of heart disease, certain types of cancer and obesity. A diet that is rich in saturated fats, found in foods such as fatty cuts of meat and meat products, full-fat dairy products, butter and some types of margarine, increases the levels of cholesterol in the blood.

Weight for weight, fat provides twice as many calories as carbohydrate or protein. There is also some evidence to suggest that calories eaten as fat are more likely to be laid down as body fat than calories from protein or carbohydrate. The good news is that these days low in fat doesn't have to mean low in taste. There are easy ways to trim the fat from your diet (see page 20) without giving up the foods you enjoy.

Sugar provides 'empty' calories – calories that provide nothing else in the way of protein, fibre, vitamins or minerals, and calories that most of us could do without. So it makes sense to cut down on it where you can. Sugar and sugary foods also increase the risk of tooth decay, especially when eaten between meals.

- Total fat should provide no more than 35% of your total calories each day. For a woman eating 2000 calories a day this amounts to 70g of fat.
- Saturated fat should provide no more than 10% of your total fat intake. For a woman eating 2000 calories a day this amounts to 21g of fat.
- Look at the nutritional labelling on food packaging to check the fat content of the food, looking particularly at the amount of saturated fat.
- Avoid adding sugar to food.

DIETARY FIBRE

Although it passes through our digestive tract unchanged, fibre is essential for a healthy digestive system.

Fibre can be divided into two groups: insoluble fibre and soluble fibre. Insoluble fibre is found mainly in wheat, wholegrain cereals, fruit and vegetables and pulses. It has the effect of holding or absorbing water, which helps to prevent constipation and diverticular disease. It also speeds up the rate at which waste material is passed through the body and this is believed to play an important role in preventing bowel cancer by reducing the length of time that cancer-causing toxins stay within the digestive system.

Soluble fibre, found in oats and oat bran, beans and pulses and some fruits, can help to lower high blood cholesterol levels and slow down the absorption of sugar into the bloodstream.

The recommended daily intake of fibre for men and women is 18g. Surveys show that only 2 out of 10 people reach this target.

EASY WAYS TO INCREASE YOUR FIBRE INTAKE:

• Choose a wholegrain cereal such as porridge, muesli or bran flakes for breakfast. Choose one that provides 3g of fibre or more per serving.

• Choose wholemeal or Granary bread. Just because bread is brown it doesn't necessarily mean that it is high in fibre – look for the words wholegrain, wholewheat or wholemeal on the label.
• Eat more beans and pulses such as lentils, red kidney beans and chickpeas.
• Eat a minimum of 5 servings of fruit and vegetables a day.
• Eat ready-to-eat dried fruit as an inbetween-meals snack or add it to your breakfast cereal.
• Use brown rather than white rice, and wholemeal pasta.

13

SALT (SODIUM CHLORIDE)

Sodium plays a vital role in the body's fluid balance as well as being involved in muscle and nerve activity. Almost all of us, however, consume far more than is good for us. A high salt intake is believed to be a major factor in the development of high blood pressure, which increases the risk of stroke and heart disease.

- Experts recommend reducing our daily salt intake to no more than 6g (equivalent to 2.4g sodium). This is only 1 teaspoon of salt, which is around half our current average intake.
- Around 80% of the sodium in our diet comes from processed foods – one small can of chicken soup, for instance, can contain over half the recommended daily amount.
- Train your tastebuds to enjoy foods with less salt. Try using herbs and spices, lemon or mustard to flavour your foods.
- As a general rule, foods that contain more than 0.5g sodium per serving are high in sodium. Foods that contain less than 0.1g sodium per serving are low in sodium. Always read the nutritional labelling on packaging.
- The **count on us...** range has strictly controlled levels of salt.

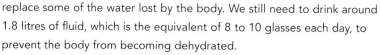

WATER

Water is vital to good health. Unlike some other nutrients, the human body does not store water so you need to drink a regular supply.

Some foods, particularly fruit and vegetables, contain quite a lot of water – a slice of watermelon, for instance, is 92% water and an apple 84% – and eating them can help

replace some of the water lost by the body. We still need to drink around 1.8 litres of fluid, which is the equivalent of 8 to 10 glasses each day, to prevent the body from becoming dehydrated.

Around 85% of our brain tissue is water – which explains why even mild dehydration can lead to problems such as headaches, lethargy, dizziness and an inability to concentrate. Long-term dehydration can lead to digestive problems, kidney problems and joint pain. Relying on thirst to tell you when you need to take a drink is not a good idea – by the time you feel thirsty your body is probably already mildly dehydrated.

- Drink at least 8 to 10 glasses (a glass is about 225ml/8fl oz) of fluid a day.
- Don't rely on thirst as a sign that you need to take a drink.
- Eating plenty of fruit and vegetables will help increase your fluid intake.
- Take water breaks rather than coffee breaks at regular intervals during the day.
- Keeping a bottle of water on your desk at work will remind you to take a drink.
- To check to see you are drinking enough fluid look at your urine – if you're drinking enough it should be a light yellow colour. Dark yellow urine is a sign you're not drinking enough.
- Drink plenty of water before, during and after taking exercise – especially in warm weather.

ALCOHOL

Alcohol is not forbidden on a diet but it is worth remembering that for most of us willpower dissolves in alcohol! A glass of wine may only be 85 calories but the trouble is that one glass easily leads to another and after a couple of drinks it's easy to forget about your good intentions to eat healthily. If you drink alcohol stay within the recommended safe guidelines which are no more than 2–3 units a day for women, 3–4 units a day for men, with 2–3 alcohol-free days during the week.

1 unit equals:
1 (125ml) glass of wine
300ml (½pint) ordinary-strength beer or cider
1 single measure (25ml) spirits
1 single measure (50ml) port or sherry

---

8 STEPS TO A HEALTHY DIET

Enjoy your food

Eat a variety of different foods

Eat the right amount to achieve a healthy weight

Eat plenty of foods rich in carbohydrates and fibre

Eat plenty of fruit and vegetables

Don't eat too many foods that contain a lot of fat

Don't have sugary foods and drinks too often

Drink alcohol sensibly

LOSING WEIGHT SAFELY

If you're trying to lose weight you're not alone. Almost 60% of adults in the UK are now classified as overweight (BMI over 25 – see page 17), and 17% of men and 21% of women are obese (BMI over 30). The number of obese people in the UK has trebled since 1990. Many nutritionists believe that the reason for this alarming rise is due not to our eating more but to our doing less. Modern technology and labour-saving devices mean that we're much less active than we used to be.

Our weight is a reflection of the balance between the energy (calories) we consume and the energy we use. Our energy intake is determined by the amount and type of food we eat. Our energy expenditure is determined by a combination of our resting metabolic rate and the amount of calories we burn in day-to-day activities.

The resting metabolic rate is the amount of energy our body needs to keep it ticking over, similar to the fuel used by a car when the engine is idling but the car is stationary.

If our energy intake equals our energy expenditure our body weight will remain the same, but if our intake exceeds our expenditure the excess energy is stored in the body as fat (see below).

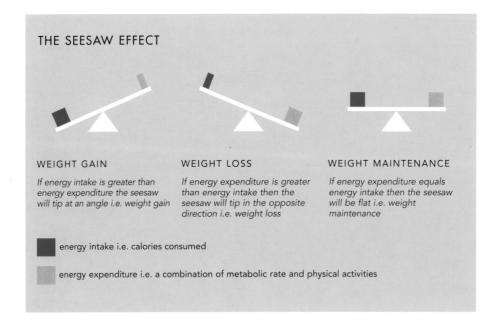

THE SEESAW EFFECT

WEIGHT GAIN
If energy intake is greater than energy expenditure the seesaw will tip at an angle i.e. weight gain

WEIGHT LOSS
If energy expenditure is greater than energy intake then the seesaw will tip in the opposite direction i.e. weight loss

WEIGHT MAINTENANCE
If energy expenditure equals energy intake then the seesaw will be flat i.e. weight maintenance

■ energy intake i.e. calories consumed

■ energy expenditure i.e. a combination of metabolic rate and physical activities

THE IDEAL RATE OF WEIGHT LOSS

Experts agree the best and safest way to lose weight is slowly and steadily – between 0.5 and 1kg (1 and 2lb) a week is the ideal rate. If you lose too much weight too quickly there is a danger of losing lean muscle tissue as well as fat. Since our basal metabolic rate (the number of calories the body needs to function) is related to the amount of lean muscle tissue we have it's a good idea to do whatever we can to preserve it.

HOW LOW SHOULD YOU GO?

The total number of calories we need to eat each day varies depending on a number of factors such as age, weight, sex, activity levels, body composition and metabolic rate. As a general guide, women need around 2000 calories a day and men need 2500. To lose 0.5kg (1lb) a week, you need to reduce your calorie intake by 500 calories a day. Diets that restrict calories too severely (fewer than 1000 calories a day for women) are not recommended.

HOW YOU SHAPE UP

Although most of us can get a pretty good idea of whether we need to lose weight or not just by looking in the mirror, if you want a more accurate assessment you can calculate your body mass index or waist circumference (see panel below).

HOW YOU SHAPE UP

BMI (Body Mass Index) = your weight (in kilograms) ÷ your height (in metres) squared. For example:-

$$\frac{60kg}{(1.65m \times 1.65m)} = 22 \qquad 1kg = 2.2lb \ 1m = 39.37in$$

Under 20	*underweight*
20–25	*healthy weight range*
25–30	*overweight*
30–40	*obese*
Over 40	*severely obese*

(Source: British Nutrition Foundation, 1999)

WAIST CIRCUMFERENCE

Men	**Women**
Waist circumference over 94cm (37in) *indicates a slight health risk*	Waist circumference over 80cm (31½in) *indicates a slight health risk*
Waist circumference over 102cm (40in) *indicates a substantial health risk*	Waist circumference over 88cm (34½in) *indicates a substantial health risk*

THE 3 MAIN REASONS THAT DIETS FAIL
Setting unrealistic goals – if you set unrealistic goals you're more likely to become disheartened and give up. Aim for a slow but steady weight loss of 0.5–1kg (1–2lb) a week. If you lose too much weight too quickly there's a danger of losing lean muscle tissue as well as fat.
Following the wrong sort of diet – however tempting they may seem, crash diets just don't work. Although you may lose weight initially, you'll find you will end up putting on not just the weight you originally lost but more.
Not eating enough – a mistake people often make is to reduce their calorie intake too severely. Overly strict diets are difficult to stick to in the long run, they're not necessary and they're not healthy. If you restrict your calories too severely the chances are you'll end up missing out on important nutrients.

UNDERSTANDING YOUR RELATIONSHIP WITH FOOD

Often we eat out of habit or to satisfy emotional needs rather than because we are hungry. We use food to celebrate, to relieve boredom, to make us feel better when we're unhappy or lonely. Certain people, places, moods and situations can also prompt us to eat.

Keeping a food diary will help you to identify these external cues. Buy a notebook and divide the pages into columns as shown below. Keep a record of everything you eat and drink and how you feel for two weeks.

FOOD DIARY					
Date and Time	Where you are	What you are doing and who you're with	How you feel (e.g. tired, unhappy, bored)	What you ate	How hungry are you? On a scale of 1–5 1=hungry 5=not hungry
Wednesday 3.30pm	At home	Nothing	Bored	Packet of crisps	5
Thursday 10.30am	At work	Trying to meet tight deadline	Stressed	Chocolate bar	4

At the end of two weeks review your diary and make a list of all the triggers that prompt you to eat when you're not really hungry.

Once you have identified these trigger factors you can start to think about solutions and ways to avoid those situations in future. Work out strategies that will help avoid or change the way you behave when faced with these triggers. If, for instance, you find you get home after work so hungry that you end up eating a family-sized pack of cheesy snacks whilst preparing the evening meal, plan ahead. Have a healthy snack such as a banana or yogurt before you leave the office so you won't feel so hungry when you get home. If your diary reveals that you use food as a way of making yourself feel better when you're unhappy or depressed make a list of non-food related activities that will help lift your spirits when you're feeling low. Rent a video, have a manicure or take a long leisurely bath rather than reaching for a chocolate bar.

GETTING FITTER

A combination of diet and exercise is by far the best way to lose weight. Exercise burns calories but it also helps develop muscle tissue. Muscle is metabolically more active than your body's fat stores (it uses more calories than fat). In other words, the more muscle you have the more calories your body burns. Exercise will also help to improve your body shape and tone and help you maintain your weight loss.

If you haven't done any exercise before, take it easy when you first start. If you start with something that is beyond your levels of fitness you're more likely to become discouraged and give up.

Exercise doesn't necessarily mean getting hot and sweaty in the gym. Making small changes to your normal routine – such as getting off the bus one stop early and walking part of the way home, or taking the stairs rather than the lift – can make a big difference. Walking briskly for 20 to 30 minutes a day, 5 days a week, will burn the equivalent of 5.4kg (12lb) of fat in a year.

Choose something you enjoy and that fits in with your lifestyle – you're more likely to stick with it.

Try to persuade a friend or family member to exercise with you. If you make a commitment to a friend you're less likely to back out.

The scales never lie but they can distort the truth because muscle tissue weighs more than fat. If you're doing a lot of exercise and building muscle tissue the scales may not move – don't be disheartened. You should notice your body becoming more toned and shapely and, most importantly, you will be healthier.

TRIMMING THE FAT

Fat provides twice as many calories as either protein or carbohydrate, which is why the most effective way of reducing calories is to limit the amount of fat you use.

• Start with low-fat ingredients – white fish, shellfish, chicken and lean meat are all good choices.

• Trim off visible fat from meat before cooking and remove the skin from poultry. Avoid red meat that has too much fat or marbling.

• Choose low-fat cooking techniques – poach, braise, steam, roast, grill or stir-fry. Marinades are a good way of adding extra flavour without fat.

• Invest in a good heavy-based non-stick pan and remember that oil expands once it gets hot – so when you're softening onions or vegetables you don't need to add as much as you might think. Use a vegetable or olive oil non-stick cooking spray for dishes that require light frying.

• You don't need fat to add flavour – use plenty of fresh herbs and spices in your cooking. Adding a squeeze of fresh lemon juice just before serving can give food a real flavour boost.

• Bulk out savoury dishes by adding plenty of vegetables. They are low in calories and provide essential vitamins.

• Use reduced- and low-fat alternatives such as reduced-fat cheese, skimmed milk and low-fat yoghurts where available.

• To make gravies and sauces creamy, add yoghurt or fromage frais rather than cream. Stir in at the end of cooking to prevent curdling.

• Using cheese with a strong flavour, such as mature Cheddar, Parmesan or Stilton, will mean that you need to use less.

• Don't be afraid to use high-fat foods such as cheese and bacon, but you will only need to use small quantities to add a lot of flavour.

• One tablespoon of French dressing contains 97 calories and almost 11g fat. Use sparingly or choose a low-fat dressing.

ESSENTIAL TIPS FOR LOSING WEIGHT FOREVER

1 / **Recognise why you overeat** – before you reach for a chocolate bar or slice of cake ask yourself if you're really hungry. Keep a food diary (see page 18) to help you identify danger times when you are more likely to overeat.

2 / **Believe you can do it** – a recent study found that people who believed they could lose weight and keep it off were more likely to succeed. Try to visualise the new, slimmer you and keep that image in your mind.

3 / Eat slowly and chew your food thoroughly – the brain takes 15 minutes to get the message that your stomach has had enough to eat. If you eat too quickly your stomach fills up before your brain knows you are full, and you end up eating too much.

4 / Never skip meals or allow yourself to get overhungry. If you do you'll be more tempted to snack and overeat at your next meal. Aim to eat three small to medium-sized meals a day plus 2 or 3 small, healthy snacks.

5 / Always eat breakfast – if you skip breakfast you're more likely to snack during the morning and overeat at lunch.

6 / Get fruity – fruit and vegetables are a dieter's best friend – they're low in calories and fat-free. Aim to eat at least 5 servings a day. Be adventurous and try something new. Look for recipes and ideas for new ways of cooking fruit or vegetables.

7 / Stack up with starches and fill up with fibre – choose fibre-rich varieties such as wholemeal bread and wholegrain cereals whenever possible. These provide slow-release energy which helps keep blood sugar levels stable.

8 / Be prepared – make sure your cupboards and freezer are full of healthy foods and have plenty of low-calorie snacks available.

9 / Don't feel that one bad day will ruin the whole diet – life is full of ups and downs, so if you do lapse on the odd bad day be a little stricter with yourself the following day.

10 / Never go shopping on an empty stomach – always write a list and stick to it! Don't buy foods you know you won't be able to resist.

11 / Don't deny yourself the foods you enjoy – just eat them in moderation.

12 / Drink at least 8 glasses of water a day – it's easy to confuse thirst with hunger. When you think you're feeling hungry try drinking a large glass of water first.

13 / Trim the fat – fat is a dieter's biggest enemy. Whenever possible, choose products that have less than 3% fat.

14 / Make use of every opportunity you can to stay active – use the stairs instead of the lift or escalator, get off the bus one stop early and walk the rest of the way home. Small changes all add up and can make a big difference.

HELPLINES/CONTACTS

The British Dietetic Association
5th Floor, Charles House, 148/9 Great Charles Street,
Queensway, Birmingham B3 3HT
Tel: 0121 200 8080
Website: www.bda.uk.com

Eating Disorders Association
103 Prince of Wales Road, Norwich NR1 1DW
Helpline: 01603 621 414 (open 9:00 to 18:30 weekdays)
Website: www.edauk.com

The British Nutrition Foundation
High Holborn House, 52–54 High Holborn,
London WC1V 6RQ
Tel: 020 7404 6504
Website: www.nutrition.org.uk

Weight Concern
Brook House, 2–16 Torrington Place, London WC1E 7HN
Tel: 020 7679 6636
Website: www.weightconcern.com

Many nutritionists consider breakfast to be the most important meal of the day, particularly for anyone watching their weight. Cutting calories by skipping breakfast is a false economy – if you miss breakfast you're much more likely

Breakfasts

to get hungry mid-morning and overeat at lunch-time. Studies show that people who eat breakfast in the morning are less likely to be overweight than those who skip it. Miss breakfast and you're also missing out on the opportunity to boost your intake of several important vitamins and minerals. People who regularly eat breakfast have been shown to have a higher intake of vitamins B_1, B_2, niacin, B_6, folic acid, B_{12}, C and D, as well as the minerals iron and calcium, when compared with those who didn't eat anything. Other studies show that people who eat breakfast are less likely to suffer from colds and flu.

Dried fruit compôte

prep 5 minutes + 3 hours soaking | serves 1

*Opposite
foreground: Dried
fruit compôte;
background:
Apple and
blueberry muesli*

50g (1¾oz) ready-to-eat dried
    fruit (apricots, figs, prunes),
    roughly chopped
2 cardamom pods, lightly crushed
100ml (3½fl oz) boiling water
juice 2 oranges, about 125ml (4fl oz)
1 x 15ml sp (1tbsp) 0% fat Greek
    style yoghurt

1. Place the fruit and crushed cardamom in
a large heatproof bowl. Pour over the water
and orange juice and leave to soak for at
least 3 hours.
2. Remove the cardamom and serve with
the yoghurt swirled in.

COOK'S TIP

• *Any type of dried fruit combination can
be used to make the compôte.*

Apple and blueberry muesli

prep 5 minutes + overnight soaking | serves 1

30g (1¼oz) count on us... muesli
75ml (2½fl oz) apple juice
1 eating apple, cored
75g (2¾oz) blueberries
    or blackberries
3 x 15ml sp (3tbsp) low-fat
    bio-yoghurt

1. Place the muesli in a bowl, pour over
the apple juice, cover and put in the
fridge to chill overnight.
2. Coarsely grate the apple and add to
the muesli. Stir in the berries and low-fat
bio-yoghurt and serve.

NUTRITION INFORMATION

per serving

calories	fat	sat fat	salt
130	0.3g	trace	trace

NUTRITION INFORMATION

per serving

calories	fat	sat fat	salt
255	3g	0.7g	0.2g

Creamy mushrooms on toast

prep 5 minutes | **cook** 10 minutes | **serves** 1

1 x 2.5ml sp (½tsp) olive oil
1–3 spring onions, optional, finely chopped
1 small clove garlic, optional, finely chopped or pressed
100g (3½oz) whole button mushrooms (or other mushrooms, quartered)
1 rasher 'less than 5% fat' bacon
1 x 15ml sp (1 tbsp) chopped fresh parsley
freshly ground black pepper, to taste
1 slice granary bread, toasted

1. Add the oil to a small, lidded, non-stick saucepan over a low heat.
2. Add the spring onion, garlic and mushrooms and stir until blended. Put a lid on the saucepan and continue cooking, shaking the pan to mix the ingredients. If necessary, add 1 x 15ml sp (1tbsp) of water.
3. Cook the mixture for 5–10 minutes or until the mushrooms have changed colour and released their juices.
4. Pan-fry the bacon quickly in a non-stick frying pan and add to the mushrooms.
5. Stir in the parsley and black pepper and serve on hot toast, topped with the bacon.

COOK'S TIPS

• *Avoid using field mushrooms in this recipe as they absorb too much oil and their juices mean the sauce becomes an unattractive black colour.*
• *To dress this dish up for dinner, you can substitute white wine for the water added during cooking, or add a little half-fat crème fraîche (1tsp adds an extra 9 calories and 1g of fat to the total for the dish).*

NUTRITION INFORMATION

per serving

calories	fat	sat fat	salt
155	4.6g	0.9g	1.2g

Ginger fruit teabread with mashed banana

(V) | **prep** 10 minutes + 2 hours soaking + 2 hours cooling | **cook** 1 hour 15 minutes | **prep ahead** 24 hours | **serves** 5 (10 slices)

50g (1¾oz) ready-to-eat dried apricots, roughly chopped
50g (1¾oz) ready-to-eat jumbo sultanas
50g (1¾oz) pitted ready-to-eat prunes, roughly chopped
300ml (½pint) strongly brewed tea without milk, allowed to cool
225g (8oz) plain white flour
2 x 5ml sp (2tsp) baking powder
1 x 5ml sp (1tsp) ground ginger
125g (4½oz) muscovado sugar
1 medium egg, beaten

for the topping (per serving)
1 small banana, mashed

1. Preheat the oven to 180°C/350°F/Gas Mark 4. Lightly grease a 900-g (2-lb) loaf tin and line the base with baking paper.
2. Put the dried fruit in a large measuring jug or bowl, pour over the tea and leave to stand for at least 2 hours, stirring occasionally.
3. Put the flour, baking powder, ginger, sugar and egg into a food processor and blend for a couple of minutes or until well mixed. Add the dried fruits and blend again until mixed.
4. Turn the mixture into the prepared tin, level the surface and brush lightly with water. Place on the centre shelf of the oven for 1¼ hours or until cooked.
5. Allow the cake to cool in the tin for 10–15 minutes. Loosen the edges with a knife and then turn out onto a wire rack to cool.
6. When cool, cut off slices and serve topped with mashed banana.

COOK'S TIP
• *Any dried fruit can be used as an alternative to the apricots and sultanas.*

NUTRITION INFORMATION
per serving

(⅕ of loaf (2 slices), topped with banana)

calories	fat	sat fat	salt
240	1.3g	0.3g	0.3g

However busy you are it's important to make the time to sit down and enjoy a proper lunch. Tempting as it is to skip meals when you're busy, if you do you're more likely to end up snacking on chocolate or biscuits later in the

Soups, salads and

afternoon. Try to include at least 1 serving of vegetables and 1 serving of fruit at lunchtime. Drinking a large glass of still or sparkling water before you start eating will help fill your stomach and reduce the risk of overeating.

light lunches

Carrot and cumin soup

V | **prep** 5 minutes | **cook** 30 minutes | **serves** 1 (*or 2 small starter portions*)

1 medium–large carrot, peeled and finely chopped
1 small clove garlic, peeled and chopped
1 medium–large shallot, peeled and finely chopped
1 ripe tomato, skinned (see COOK'S TIP) and chopped
1 x 2.5ml sp (½tsp) ground cumin
200ml (7fl oz) vegetable stock
1 bouquet garni (see COOK'S TIP)
freshly ground black pepper, to taste
2 x 5ml sp (2tsp) dry sherry (optional)
1 x 15ml sp (1tbsp) half-fat crème fraîche (optional), to serve
pinch of cumin, to garnish

1. Put all the ingredients except the sherry and crème fraîche in a lidded saucepan.
2. Bring to simmering point over a high heat, then reduce the heat and simmer for
30 minutes or until the vegetables are tender. Cool slightly and remove the bouquet garni.
3. Pour the soup into an electric blender and purée until smooth.
4. Return to the saucepan, add the sherry, if using, and reheat. Taste for seasoning. Serve
with a swirl of crème fraîche, if using, and a pinch of cumin.

COOK'S TIPS

• *To skin a tomato, make a cross with a knife across the stalk end, pop into boiling water
for a few minutes, drain, then slip off the skin.*
• *To make a bouquet garni, tie a bay leaf and a few sprigs of parsley and thyme in a bunch or in a
piece of muslin.*

PREPARE AHEAD

• *Complete to the end of step 3, cool, cover and refrigerate for up to 24 hours.
Continue with step 4.*

NUTRITION INFORMATION

per serving
(including the sherry and crème fraîche)

calories	fat	sat fat	salt
135	4.2g	0.4g	0.6g

Spiced lentil and vegetable soup

(V) | **prep** 5 minutes | **cook** 50 minutes–1 hour | **serves** 1

1 x 5ml sp (1tsp) vegetable or olive oil
1 x 5ml sp (1tsp) mild curry paste
1 clove garlic, peeled and crushed or finely chopped
350ml (12fl oz) vegetable stock
1 medium onion, chopped
30g (1¼oz) dried red lentils
1 medium carrot, peeled and chopped
1 small parsnip or potato, peeled and chopped
1 medium stalk celery, chopped
1 x 5ml sp (1tsp) tomato purée

1. Heat the oil in a lidded, non-stick saucepan, add the curry paste and garlic and stir over a low heat for 1 minute.
2. Add the stock and stir to combine, then add the rest of the ingredients and bring to a simmer over a medium-high heat.
3. Turn the heat down, put the lid on and cook for 40–50 minutes or until the lentils are tender.
4. Remove half or all the soup from the pan (according to taste – see COOK'S TIP) and purée in an electric blender. Return the soup to the pan and reheat gently to serve.

COOK'S TIP
• *By blending only half the quantity, you get a nice thick soup, which is still chunky.*

NUTRITION INFORMATION

per serving

calories	fat	sat fat	salt
280	6.8g	0.1g	0.8g

35

Roast mushroom and garlic soup with wholemeal croûtons

(V) | **prep** 2 minutes | **cook** 30–40 minutes | **serves** 1

2 open-cap mushrooms, wiped clean
2 cloves garlic, peeled
1 slice wholemeal bread, cut into small cubes
1 x 5ml sp (1tsp) olive oil
7g (¼oz) dried porcini mushrooms
250ml (9fl oz) vegetable stock
1 x 5ml sp (1tsp) fresh thyme leaves
1 x 5ml sp (1tsp) vegetarian Worcestershire sauce
freshly ground black pepper, to taste
1 x 5ml sp (1tsp) half-fat crème fraîche, optional
few sprigs of thyme, to garnish

1. Preheat the oven to 180°C/350°F/Gas Mark 5.
2. Loosely wrap the open-cap mushrooms and garlic in foil and place in the oven. Bake for 10 minutes, open the foil, and bake for a further 5 minutes.
3. To prepare the croûtons, drizzle the bread cubes with 1 teaspoon olive oil, place on a baking sheet and bake for 10–15 minutes or until golden brown.
4. Meanwhile, put the porcini mushrooms, stock and thyme leaves in a lidded saucepan.
5. When the open-cap mushrooms are cooked, remove from the oven, slice and add them to the saucepan with the Worcestershire sauce, roasted garlic, the mushroom juices and pepper.
6. Cover and simmer for 15 minutes over a low heat.
7. Leave to cool slightly and purée half the soup in an electric blender for a few seconds. Return to the pan and reheat gently. Stir in the crème fraîche and adjust the pepper to taste.
8. Transfer to a bowl, sprinkle over the croûtons and sprigs of thyme and serve.

COOK'S TIP
• *Field mushrooms will add extra flavour if you can get them.*

NUTRITION INFORMATION
per serving

calories	fat	sat fat	salt
140	5.4g	1.2g	1.0g

Spiced chicken and apricot salad

prep 10 minutes | **cook** 10 minutes | **serves** 1

25g (1oz) brown basmati rice
1 x 15ml sp (1tbsp) plain low-fat yoghurt
2 x 5ml sp (2tsp) mango chutney
1 x 5ml sp (1tsp) mild curry paste
75g (2¾oz) cooked skinless chicken breast, diced
2 spring onions, shredded
½ stick celery, finely chopped
25g (1oz) ready-to-eat dried apricots, roughly chopped
25g (1oz) fresh baby spinach leaves

1. Rinse the rice in cold water and put in a small saucepan. Cover with water and bring to the boil, reduce the heat, cover and simmer for 10 minutes or until just tender. Drain well then turn the rice into a bowl.
2. Mix the yoghurt, mango chutney and curry paste together.
3. Add the chicken, spring onions, celery, apricots and yoghurt mixture to the cooked rice. Stir the mixture well.
4. Serve warm on a bed of baby spinach.

COOK'S TIP

• *Brown rice adds more fibre and B vitamins, but if you prefer you can use white rice. Different types of rice will have different cooking times, so follow the instructions on the packet.*

NUTRITION INFORMATION
per serving

calories	fat	sat fat	salt
290	6.4g	1.3g	0.9g

Lentil and goat's cheese salad

V | **prep** 10 minutes | **cook** 20–30 minutes | **serves** 1

25g (1oz) dried Puy lentils
1 bay leaf
2 spring onions, finely chopped
50g (1¾oz) red pepper, diced
1 x 15ml sp (1tbsp) chopped fresh parsley
100g (3½oz) cherry tomatoes, sliced in half

for the dressing
1 x 5ml sp (1tsp) olive oil
1 x 5ml sp (1tsp) balsamic vinegar
1 x 2.5ml sp (½tsp) runny honey
1 clove garlic, peeled and crushed or finely chopped
50g (1¾oz) rocket
30g (1¼oz) goat's cheese, sliced or crumbled

1. Rinse the lentils and put in a medium-sized saucepan. Add the bay leaf and cover with plenty of cold water, bring to the boil then reduce the heat and simmer for 20–30 minutes or until the lentils are tender.
2. Drain the lentils and transfer to a bowl. Add the spring onions, red pepper, parsley and cherry tomatoes. Mix well.
3. Whisk together the oil, vinegar, honey and garlic and stir into the lentils. Serve on a bed of rocket, with the goat's cheese sprinkled over.

COOK'S TIP
• *If time is short, replace the dried lentils with 75g (2¾oz), drained weight, canned cooked lentils.*

NUTRITION INFORMATION
per serving

calories	fat	sat fat	salt
220	9.3g	3.8g	0.4g

Tunisian poached egg

V | **prep** 5 minutes | **cook** 20 minutes | **serves** 1

1 x 5ml sp (1tsp) olive oil
1 small green pepper, deseeded and thinly sliced
1 small red or yellow pepper, deseeded and thinly sliced
1 small onion or large shallot, peeled and thinly sliced
200g (7oz) canned tomatoes, chopped
1 x 5ml sp (1tsp) ground cumin
freshly ground black pepper, to taste
1 small egg
pinch of sweet paprika (optional)
2 M&S mini pitta breads or 1 slice wholemeal or granary bread, toasted

1. Heat the oil in a non-stick frying pan and sauté the peppers and onion over a medium-high heat for about 5 minutes, stirring occasionally, or until they are soft and turning golden.
2. Add the tomatoes, cumin and seasoning and stir to combine, then cook for a further 5 minutes.
3. Meanwhile, heat water in a frying pan to a depth of 3cm (1¼inches) to simmering point, and break the egg into the pan. Keep the water barely simmering and poach the egg for 3 minutes or until the white is cooked.
4. Serve the peppers in an individual gratin dish with the egg on top and sprinkle with the paprika, if using, and season to taste. Serve with warm pitta bread or toast.

COOK'S TIPS
• *Make sure the egg is very fresh or it will not poach well.*
• *If you have time, or if you are already using the oven, at the end of step 1 you can transfer the peppers into an ovenproof gratin dish and break the egg into a well in the middle of them. Then cook at 190°C/375°F/Gas Mark 5 for 10 minutes or until the egg is cooked but still soft.*

NUTRITION INFORMATION

per serving

calories	fat	sat fat	salt
290	10g	2.3g	0.9g

43

Thai fish cakes with sweet chilli dipping sauce

prep 5 minutes + 30 minutes chilling | **cook** 6 minutes | **serves** 1 (makes 2 cakes)

for the fish cakes
100g (3½oz) skinless cod or haddock fillet
1 spring onion, finely chopped
¼ red chilli, deseeded and finely chopped
1 x 1.5ml sp (¼tsp) finely chopped root ginger
1 small clove garlic, peeled and crushed or finely chopped
2 x 5ml sp (2tsp) lime juice
1 x 15ml sp (1tbsp) chopped fresh coriander leaves
1 x 5ml sp (1tsp) vegetable oil

for the chilli sauce
1 x 2.5ml sp (½tsp) finely chopped root ginger
½ mild red chilli, deseeded and finely chopped
2 x 5ml sp (2tsp) soft brown sugar
1 x 2.5ml sp (½tsp) light soy sauce
1 x 15ml sp (1tbsp) dry sherry

for the salad garnish
½ small carrot, finely sliced into strips
2 spring onions, finely sliced into strips
3cm (1¼inches) cucumber, finely sliced into strips
lime wedges, to garnish

1. Put all the fish cake ingredients except the oil in a food processor and blend until smooth.
2. With wet hands divide the mixture in half and shape into 2 fish cakes. Put on a plate, cover and chill for at least 30 minutes.
3. Prepare the salad garnish.
4. Put all the sauce ingredients in a food processor and blend until smooth (or shake them up in a lidded jar).
5. Heat the oil in a shallow, non-stick frying pan and cook the fish cakes over a medium heat for about 3 minutes. Turn and cook for a further 3 minutes or until firm. Serve garnished with salad, lime wedges, and with the sauce on the side.

COOK'S TIP
• *Make sure the fish cake mixture is well blended to ensure the fish cakes hold their shape while cooking.*

NUTRITION INFORMATION
per serving (i.e. 2 cakes)

calories	fat	sat fat	salt
200	4g	0.6g	0.7g

Healthy eating doesn't have to mean spending hours in the kitchen. With a little thought and forward planning there are plenty of simple dishes that you can assemble and cook in a matter of minutes. However, if you do have the time

Meat and fish main

available, preparing a meal in the evening can be a relaxing and creative end to the day. Variety may be the spice of life but it's also the key to a healthy, well-balanced diet so don't fall into the trap of eating the same meals week in week out. If time is at a premium it helps to be organised – make sure your cupboards and freezer are well stocked and plan ahead: try to write a menu for the week at the weekend when you have a little more time. Remember, vegetables are a dieter's best friend so supplement your main dish with plenty of vegetables or salad.

courses

Chicken and pine nuts with saffron couscous and lemon dressing

prep 10 minutes │ **cook** 10 minutes, including soaking time │ **serves** 1

1–2 strands saffron
50g (1¾oz), dry weight, couscous
2 x 5ml sp (2tsp) sultanas
125ml (4fl oz) boiling hot chicken or vegetable stock

for the dressing
1 x 5ml sp (1tsp) finely chopped fresh coriander leaves
juice of ½ lemon
1 x 5ml sp (1tsp) olive oil

l x 100g (3½oz) chicken breast fillet, cut into 8 strips
25g (1oz) sweetcorn kernels
1 x 5ml sp (1tsp) pine nuts
10 cherry tomatoes, quartered
2 spring onions, trimmed and chopped
fresh coriander leaves, to garnish

1. Put the saffron, couscous and sultanas in a heatproof bowl and pour over the hot stock. Stir once and allow to stand for 15 minutes.
2. Meanwhile, whisk together the dressing ingredients.
3. Brown the chicken strips on all sides in a non-stick frying pan over a high heat for about 4 minutes.
4. Reduce the heat to medium, add the sweetcorn and pine nuts and cook for a further 2 minutes, stirring once or twice. Remove the chicken from the frying pan and set aside.
5. Fluff up the couscous with a fork and add to the frying pan with the tomatoes, dressing and spring onions. Heat for 1 minute, or until warmed through, stirring gently.
6. Spoon onto a plate, top with the chicken slices and garnish with coriander.

NUTRITION INFORMATION

per serving

calories	fat	sat fat	salt
380	11.7g	2.5g	1.5g

Chicken with mushroom stuffing and butternut squash

prep 30 minutes | **cook** 50 minutes | **serves** 2

for the stuffing
7g (¼oz) dried mushrooms
100ml (3½fl oz) boiling water
1 x 5ml sp (1tsp) olive oil
50g (1¾oz) fresh brown-cap mushrooms, finely chopped
25g (1oz) 95% fat-free soft cheese
2 x 125g (4½oz) skinless chicken breasts
2 slices Parma ham, trimmed of any fat

for the squash
625g (1lb 6oz), peeled weight, butternut squash, deseeded and cut into
  2-cm (¾-inch) chunks
2 x 15ml sp (2tbsp) chopped fresh rosemary
2 x 15ml sp (2tbsp) chopped fresh oregano
freshly ground black pepper, to taste
1 x 5ml sp (1tsp) olive oil

1. Preheat the oven to 180°C/350°F/Gas Mark 4.
2. Wash the dried mushrooms, pour over the boiling water and leave to stand for 5 minutes. Drain and finely chop.
3. Heat the oil in a non-stick pan, add the fresh and dried mushrooms and cook over a medium heat for 10 minutes or until they are beginning to brown and any liquid has evaporated. Allow to cool.
4. Put the soft cheese in a bowl, stir in the mushrooms and season to taste. Mix well.
5. Using a sharp knife, make a slit lengthways in each chicken breast to form a pocket. Spoon in the mushroom mixture. Wrap 1 slice of ham around each breast and enclose in foil to make a parcel.
6. Put the chunks of squash into a roasting dish. Add the chopped herbs and pepper then drizzle with the oil. Stir to coat.
7. Place the chicken parcel on top of the butternut squash and bake for 30 minutes. Remove the foil and return the chicken and squash to the oven for a further 10 minutes, or until the chicken is cooked. Serve immediately.

COOK'S TIPS
• You can replace the butternut squash with any other type of squash or pumpkin.
• For a different effect you can purée the cooked squash and serve it topped with the chicken.

NUTRITION INFORMATION
per serving

calories	fat	sat fat	salt
325	9.5g	2.4g	0.9g

51

Spanish rice with pork and peppers

prep 5 minutes | **cook** 40–50 minutes | **serves** 1

1 x 2.5ml sp (½tsp) olive oil
75g (2¾oz) lean pork tenderloin, cut into small cubes
1 small onion, or 2 shallots, peeled and finely chopped
1 clove garlic, peeled and chopped
1 red or orange pepper, deseeded and chopped into 1-cm (½-inch) squares
200g (7oz) canned tomatoes, chopped
1 x 15ml sp (1tbsp) chopped fresh parsley
pinch of saffron strands
60g (2¼oz), dry weight, brown basmati rice
230ml (8fl oz) chicken or vegetable stock
freshly ground black pepper, to taste

1. Heat the oil in a heavy-based, lidded, non-stick frying pan and brown the pork on all sides on a high heat. Remove with a slotted spoon and keep warm.
2. Reduce the heat to medium-high and add the onion, garlic and pepper, and stir-fry for a few minutes until everything is soft and turning golden.
3. Return the meat to the pan and add the tomatoes, parsley, saffron, rice and stock, and season to taste. Stir well to combine and to break up the tomatoes a little, and bring to a simmer. Turn the heat down to low and put the lid on.
4. Simmer for 30–40 minutes or until the rice is tender, and all the stock is absorbed. (If the rice is not cooked but the dish looks dry, add a little more hot water.)

COOK'S TIPS
• *A good-quality, heavy-based pan prevents the rice from sticking or burning as it cooks.*
• *You could use cooked gammon instead of pork, but bear in mind that gammon is quite salty.*
• *Brown rice adds more fibre and B vitamins, but if you prefer you can use white rice or easy-cook brown rice, following the cooking instructions on the packet.*

NUTRITION INFORMATION

per serving

calories	fat	sat fat	salt
430	10.2g	2.6g	1.4g

Beef en daube with mustard mash

prep 10 minutes | **cook** 45 minutes–1 hour | **serves** 2

2 x 5ml sp (2tsp) vegetable oil
225g (8oz) extra-lean braising steak, cut into 8 pieces
10 small shallots, peeled but left whole
1 clove garlic, peeled and crushed
1 medium tomato, chopped
100g (3½oz) mushrooms, finely sliced
150ml (¼pint) red wine
100ml (3½fl oz) chicken stock
1 small bouquet garni
freshly ground black pepper, to taste
1 x 5ml sp (1tsp) cornflour

for the mustard mash
2 medium floury potatoes, peeled and sliced
25ml (¾fl oz) skimmed milk, heated
1 x 5ml sp (1tsp) Dijon mustard, to taste

1. Preheat the oven to 180°C/350°F/Gas Mark 4.
2. Heat the oil in a heavy-based flame-proof casserole. Add the meat and shallots and cook over a high heat, stirring, for 4–5 minutes to brown the meat on all sides. Add the garlic, tomato, mushrooms, wine and stock, and tuck the bouquet garni well in.
3. Bring to a simmer on the hob, cover and transfer to the oven to cook for 45–60 minutes, or until everything is tender.
4. About 30 minutes before the beef is ready, place the potatoes in boiling water and simmer for 20 minutes or until just tender. Remove from heat, drain well and put in a bowl. Add the milk and mash well. Stir in the mustard to taste, and keep warm.
5. Use a slotted spoon to remove the meat and vegetables to a warmed serving dish. Cook the sauce on the hob over a high heat until reduced by half. Reduce the heat, remove the bouquet garni and check the seasoning.
6. Add the cornflour to the sauce, mixed with a little cold water to form a paste, stirring well, and bring back to a simmer. Pour the sauce over the meat and serve with the mustard mash.

COOK'S TIP
• *You could add some ready-cooked pulses, such as black-eyed beans, to the beef if you like. This isn't traditional but it adds extra fibre and bulk.*

NUTRITION INFORMATION

per serving

calories	fat	sat fat	salt
330	6.4g	1.6g	1.3g

55

Chilli beef with black-eyed beans

prep 10 minutes | **cook** 1 hour | **serves** 1

1 x 5ml sp (1tsp) olive oil
1 small onion, peeled and finely chopped
1 clove garlic, peeled and crushed or finely chopped
1 small green pepper, chopped into 1-cm (½-inch) squares
75g (2¾oz) extra-lean braising steak, cut into very small pieces
1 x 5ml sp (1tsp) concentrated vegetable stock
2 x 5ml sp (2tsp) tomato purée
½ green chilli, to taste, deseeded and finely chopped
50g (1¾oz) canned black-eyed beans (or kidney beans), drained and rinsed
100g (3½oz) canned tomatoes, chopped
1 x 2.5ml sp (½tsp) chilli sauce
freshly ground black pepper, to taste
50g (1¾oz) white rice
2 x 5ml sp (2tsp) chopped fresh coriander leaves (optional), to garnish

1. Heat the oil in a non-stick frying pan and sauté the onion, garlic and pepper over a medium heat for 2–3 minutes until the onion is soft and just turning golden.
2. Add the beef and cook, stirring, until browned on all sides.
3. Add the remaining ingredients and season to taste. Stir well, bring to a simmer, cover and reduce the heat.
4. Cook for 30 minutes, then check the dish for heat, seasoning and dryness. Add extra chilli sauce, very finely chopped fresh chilli or ready-chopped chillies from a jar if it is not hot enough for you, and add water if the sauce looks too dry.
5. Cook for a further 25–30 minutes until the meat is completely tender. Meanwhile, cook the rice according to the instructions on the packet. Drain and transfer the cooked rice to a warm plate, spoon over the sauce and serve garnished with the coriander, if using.

COOK'S TIPS
• *Chillies vary a great deal in their hotness – it is always best to introduce them cautiously. You can always add more later.*
• *You can make a similar dish using cubed chicken fillet and chicken stock, but the cooking time will need to be reduced to about 30 minutes.*

NUTRITION INFORMATION
per serving

calories	fat	sat fat	salt
445	8.5g	2.1g	1.2g

Nasi goreng

prep 10 minutes | **cook** 20 minutes | **serves** 2

100g (3½oz) basmati rice
1 x 5ml sp (1tsp) vegetable oil or olive oil
1 small egg, beaten
1 x 5ml sp (1tsp) sesame oil
100g (3½oz) turkey fillet, cut into thin, bite-sized lengths
1 medium carrot, peeled and cut into thin, bite-sized lengths
4 spring onions, trimmed and chopped
2 cloves garlic, peeled and crushed
1 hot red chilli, deseeded and chopped
100g (3½oz) peeled, cooked prawns
50g (1¾oz) beansprouts
2 x 5ml sp (2tsp) soy sauce
pinch of caster sugar
chicken stock or water, as necessary

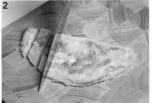

1. Bring 250ml (9fl oz) water to the boil in a lidded saucepan and tip in the rice. Return to the boil then lower the heat to a simmer. Cover the pan and cook until the rice is tender and all the water absorbed – about 10–15 minutes.
2. Meanwhile, heat the groundnut oil in an individual, non-stick omelette pan (or small frying pan). Make the omelette by adding the beaten egg and, when almost set, fold in half then turn out and slice thinly.
3. When the rice is nearly cooked, heat the sesame oil in a wok or large non-stick frying pan and stir-fry the turkey pieces for 1 minute over a high heat. Add the carrot, spring onions, garlic and chilli, and stir-fry for a further 2 minutes.
4. Reduce the heat, add the cooked rice to the frying pan with the prawns, beansprouts, soy sauce and sugar and stir gently for 1–2 minutes. If the mixture sticks, add a little chicken stock or water.
5. Arrange the omelette slices on top and serve immediately.

NUTRITION INFORMATION

per serving

calories	fat	sat fat	salt
385	7.3g	1.4g	1.7g

Prawn risotto

prep 10 minutes | **cook** 25 minutes | **serves** 2

200ml (7fl oz) hot vegetable or fish stock
100ml (3½fl oz) hot water
100ml (3½fl oz) white wine
1 x 5ml sp (1tsp) butter
2 shallots, finely chopped
1 stick celery, finely chopped
100g (3½oz) arborio or other risotto rice
freshly ground black pepper, to taste
150g (5½oz) frozen prawns, defrosted
4 x 5ml sp (4tsp) chopped fresh parsley
1 x 15ml sp (1tbsp) half-fat crème fraîche
dash of lemon juice
1 x 5ml sp (1tsp) fresh Parmesan shavings, to serve

1. Heat the butter in a medium non-stick frying pan over a medium heat. When the butter is hot, add the shallots and celery, and cook, stirring continuously for 3–4 minutes until soft.
2. Add the rice and seasoning to the frying pan and stir well to coat the rice. Mix the stock and the water. Add just enough of the stock and water mixture to cover the rice and continue to cook, stirring frequently, until it is almost completely absorbed. Continue adding the stock and water in this way until it is almost completely absorbed. Add the wine and continue cooking until that is absorbed.
3. Stir the prawns and half the parsley into the risotto and heat through.
4. Add the crème fraîche and lemon juice, stir and serve immediately with the cheese and the remaining parsley sprinkled over. Accompany with a large mixed side salad with an oil-free French dressing.

COOK'S TIP

• *Instead of the prawns you could use the same quantity of mixed seafood – crabmeat, mussels, squid, etc. If using fresh uncooked prawns, add them for the last 3 minutes of cooking.*

NUTRITION INFORMATION

per serving

calories	fat	sat fat	salt
340	6.4g	1.9g	1.5g

Mediterranean swordfish sauté with tagliatelle

prep 10 minutes | **cook** 35–40 minutes | **serves** 2

1 x 5ml sp (1tsp) olive oil
1 red onion, finely chopped
1 red pepper, diced
1 clove garlic, peeled and crushed or finely chopped
large pinch of dried chilli flakes
1 x 5ml sp (1tsp) ground coriander
1 x 5ml sp (1tsp) ground cumin
400g (14oz) canned tomatoes, chopped
1 x 15ml sp (1tbsp) tomato purée
50ml (2fl oz) red wine
freshly ground black pepper, to taste
250g (9oz) swordfish fillet, cubed
2 small courgettes, thinly sliced
100g (3½oz) dried tagliatelle or pasta shapes, to serve

1. Heat the oil in a large, non-stick, lidded pan. Add the onion, pepper, garlic, chilli, coriander and cumin and cook for 5 minutes or until onions are beginning to soften. Add the tomatoes, tomato purée and wine and season to taste. Bring to the boil, then simmer for about 20 minutes.
2. Add the swordfish and the courgettes to the rest of the ingredients and stir to combine. Bring to simmering point, cover and cook for 10–12 minutes or until the sauce is reduced by about half and the courgettes are tender.
3. Meanwhile, cook the tagliatelle according to the packet instructions, then drain. When the sauce is cooked, pour over the pasta. Serve with a green salad.

COOK'S TIPS

• *Any firm white fish will do instead of swordfish – cod and monkfish are both lower in fat and calories.*
• *You can omit the wine if you wish and add a little fish stock or water instead (fewer calories but the fish stock is higher in salt).*
• *Canned or bottled sweet peppers are quick and easy and give an excellent flavour but you could use one whole yellow pepper instead. Deseed, halve and roast or grill it until tender before slicing.*

NUTRITION INFORMATION

per serving

calories	fat	sat fat	salt
445	8.6g	1.6g	0.8g

For various reasons more and more people are choosing not to eat meat or fish. The modern approach to vegetarian cooking and the greater variety and availability of meat-free alternatives means that

Vegetarian main

many more people are choosing to eat at least a couple of meat-free meals during the week. Gone are the days when vegetarian food was considered cranky and boring. Although a vegetarian diet can be a very healthy and balanced way of eating, it often requires a little more thought and planning. The key to a healthy diet – whether you're vegetarian or not – is to eat a variety of foods. The greater the variety of foods you eat, the better chance you'll have of getting the full range of nutrients your body needs. If you cut out meat it's important to make sure that you eat other foods that provide the vitamins and minerals which you would normally get from meat. Meat is an important source of the minerals iron and zinc. If you also cut out dairy products you'll need to ensure you get enough calcium and vitamin B_{12}.

courses

Vegetable and potato-topped pie

V | prep 5 minutes | cook 50 minutes | serves 2

500g (1lb 2oz), peeled weight, potatoes, cut into chunks
2 x 15ml sp (2tbsp) semi-skimmed milk
1 x 5ml sp (1tsp) olive oil
1 small onion, finely chopped
40g (1½oz) dried brown lentils (see COOK'S TIPS)
1 clove garlic, peeled and chopped
1 stick celery, finely chopped
50g (1¾oz) brown-cap mushrooms, finely chopped
1 medium carrot, finely chopped
100ml (3½fl oz) vegetable stock
2 x 5ml sp (2tsp) vegetarian Worcestershire sauce
400g (14oz) canned chopped tomatoes with herbs
1 x 5ml sp (1tsp) dried mixed herbs
freshly ground black pepper, to taste
25g (1oz) half-fat Cheddar cheese, grated

1. Preheat the oven to 190°C/375°F/Gas Mark 5.
2. Put the potatoes in a saucepan with water to cover, bring to the boil then simmer for 15 minutes or until tender. Drain and mash the potatoes with the skimmed milk. Set aside.
3. While the potatoes are cooking, heat the oil in a non-stick frying pan and sauté the onion over a medium heat for a few minutes, stirring occasionally, to soften.
4. Add the lentils, garlic and celery to the frying pan and stir, then add the mushrooms, carrot, stock, Worcestershire sauce, herbs and tomatoes and stir everything well to combine. Bring to a simmer, cover and cook gently for 25 minutes or until you have a rich sauce and the lentils are tender. If the mixture looks too dry during cooking, add a little more stock or water. Taste and season with black pepper if necessary.
5. Spoon the lentil mixture into a two-portion baking dish and level the top. Spoon over the mashed potato and sprinkle with the cheese.
6. Bake for 15 minutes or until the potatoes are golden.

COOK'S TIPS
• *The lentil sauce can be used also as a topping for pasta, rice or baked potatoes. Once made, you can freeze it in single-portion dishes as a handy stand-by.*
• *If time is short, replace the dried lentils with 120g (4¼oz), drained weight, canned cooked lentils and reduce the cooking time by 15 minutes.*

NUTRITION INFORMATION

per serving

calories	fat	sat fat	salt
370	5.2g	1.7g	0.8g

Spinach and mushroom pancakes

Ⓥ │ **prep** 15 minutes │ **cook** 25–30 minutes │ **serves** 2

for the filling
2 x 5ml sp (2tsp) vegetable oil
350g (12oz) button or brown-cap mushrooms, roughly chopped
200ml (7fl oz) vegetable stock
275g (9½oz) frozen spinach, defrosted and squeezed dry
freshly ground black pepper, to taste
2 x 15ml (2tbsp) half-fat crème fraîche

for the pancakes (makes 8)
1 small egg
100g (3½oz) plain flour
1 x 15ml sp (1tbsp) finely chopped fresh parsley
300ml (½pint) skimmed milk
low-fat oil spray

1. First, make the filling. Heat the vegetable oil in a non-stick frying pan. Add the mushrooms and cook, stirring, for about 5 minutes.
2. Add the stock, spinach and seasoning. Reduce the heat slightly and cook for 10 minutes or until the liquid is thick and syrupy.
3. Meanwhile, make the pancakes. Put the egg, flour, parsley and milk in a blender and blend until smooth.
4. Spray a 20-cm (8-inch) heavy-based, non-stick frying pan with oil and heat until just smoking. Ladle a little of the batter onto the base of the pan and tilt until the whole of the base is thinly coated. Cook the pancake for 1 minute and then flip over and cook the other side for 1 minute.
5. Put the pancake on a plate over a pan of gently simmering water to keep warm, and continue making pancakes until all the batter is used up.
6. When the mushrooms are ready, stir in the reduced-fat crème fraîche. Spoon one-eighth of the filling into the centre of each pancake. Fold each pancake in half and serve with steamed vegetables, such as broccoli.

COOK'S TIPS
• *Making your own pancakes, rather than relying on shop-bought ones, halves the fat in this dish.*
• *You can freeze any excess pancakes in single portions, then reheat them in a non-stick frying pan.*

NUTRITION INFORMATION
per serving (i.e. 4 pancakes)

calories	fat	sat fat	salt
324	10.4g	1.6g	0.4g

Moroccan vegetable tagine

V | prep 5 minutes | cook 45 minutes | serves 2

1 x 5ml sp (1tsp) olive oil
1 medium onion, peeled and chopped
1 clove garlic, chopped
1 x 2.5ml sp (½tsp) ground aniseed
2 green cardamom pods, 'bruised' by lightly rolling with a rolling pin
½ red chilli, deseeded and finely chopped
300ml (½pint) hot vegetable stock
200g (7oz) canned tomatoes, chopped
50g (1¾oz), peeled weight, turnip or parsnip or swede or pumpkin, diced
1 medium potato, diced
1 small carrot, diced
75g (2¾oz), drained weight, canned chickpeas, rinsed
½ cinnamon stick
1 small courgette, diced
30g (1¼oz) dates, chopped
60g (2¼oz) ready-to-eat dried apricots, chopped

for the couscous
50g (1¾oz) couscous
100ml (3½fl oz) hot vegetable stock

1. Heat the oil in a large, lidded, non-stick saucepan over a medium heat. Add the onion and garlic and cook for about 5 minutes, or until soft. Reduce the heat, add the spices and cook for 1 minute, stirring.
2. Add the hot stock, tomatoes, turnip, potato, carrot, chickpeas and cinnamon and bring to the boil. Reduce the heat, cover and simmer for 30 minutes, stirring occasionally.
3. Add the courgette, dates and apricots to the saucepan, plus a little water if needed. Replace the lid and cook for a further 15 minutes or until the fruit has absorbed the liquid.
4. Meanwhile, prepare the couscous according to the instructions on the package using the hot stock. Fork through to separate the grains, then transfer to a warm dish and serve with the sauce.

COOK'S TIP
• *This sauce becomes even tastier if stored refrigerated for 1–2 days before eating.*

NUTRITION INFORMATION
per serving

calories	fat	sat fat	salt
340	4.2g	0.5g	0.6g

Autumn vegetable gratin

Ⓥ | **prep** 10 minutes | **cook** 30–35 minutes | **serves** 1

200g (7oz) canned chopped tomatoes
50g (1¾oz) closed-cap mushrooms, sliced
50g (1¾oz) broad beans, shelled weight, fresh or frozen
100g (3½oz), peeled weight, butternut squash, cut into 1-cm (½-inch) slices,
   then quartered
1 medium courgette, cut into ½-cm (¼-inch) slices
2 spring onions, finely chopped
freshly ground black pepper, to taste
few fresh basil leaves (optional)
15g (½oz) reduced-fat hard cheese, such as mature Cheddar, or a vegetarian
   Parmesan or Pecorino
1 x 15ml sp (1tbsp) fresh breadcrumbs

1. Put the tomatoes, mushrooms, beans and squash into a saucepan, bring to a simmer,
cover and simmer over a low heat for 15 minutes. Add the courgette and spring onions and
cook for a further 5–10 minutes, or until tender, adding a very little water if the chopped
tomatoes don't cover all the vegetables.
2. Season to taste, stir in the basil and then tip the mixture into an individual gratin dish
and smooth out.
3. Mix together the cheese and breadcrumbs and sprinkle over the top. Brown under a hot
grill for 1–2 minutes until golden. Serve immediately.

COOK'S TIP
• *Fresh or frozen sweetcorn can be used instead of broad beans.*

NUTRITION INFORMATION

per serving

calories	fat	sat fat	salt
180	3.9g	1.6g	0.5g

Mediterranean vegetables with goat's cheese and penne

 | **prep** 5 minutes | **cook** 15–20 minutes | **serves** 1

50g (1¾oz) dried penne pasta

for the chargrilled vegetables
1 small red pepper, deseeded and cut into bite-sized chunks
1 small courgette, cut into bite-sized slices
1 small red onion, cut into wedges
1 x 5ml sp (1tsp) olive oil
freshly ground black pepper, to taste

for the dressing
2 x 5ml sp (2tsp) balsamic vinegar
1 x 5ml sp (1tsp) lemon juice
1 x 5ml sp (1tsp) freshly torn basil leaves

35g (1¼oz) goat's cheese, crumbled
few basil leaves, to garnish
12 cherry tomatoes, halved
3 pitted black olives, halved

1. Put a saucepan of water on to boil and preheat the grill to medium-high. Cook the pasta according to the packet instructions.
2. Arrange the pepper, courgette and onion on a non-stick baking tray, brush with the oil and season with black pepper. Grill for about 5 minutes. Turn the pieces and continue grilling for a further 5 minutes or until tender.
3. When the pasta is cooked, drain well and transfer to a serving bowl. Stir in the cherry tomatoes, olives and the chargrilled vegetables with their oil and juices.
4. Beat together the dressing ingredients and stir into the pasta. Crumble over the goat's cheese, garnish with basil and serve.

COOK'S TIPS
• *For a change, try adding a couple of drained canned artichoke hearts or fresh asparagus to the vegetables.*
• *Ideal served with a mixed green salad.*

NUTRITION INFORMATION
per serving

calories	fat	sat fat	salt
370	11.6g	4.3g	1.3g

Quick mushroom risotto

Ⓥ | **prep** 5 minutes + 30 minutes soaking | **cook** 30 minutes | **serves** 1

1 x 15ml sp (1tbsp) dried porcini mushrooms
1 x 5ml sp (1tsp) olive oil
1 x 5ml sp (1tsp) butter
½ medium onion, peeled and finely chopped
1 small clove garlic, peeled and finely chopped
150g (5½oz) mixed fresh mushrooms (e.g. chestnut, shiitake, button)
freshly ground black pepper, to taste
60g (2¼oz) arborio or other risotto rice
1 small courgette, chopped
200ml (7fl oz) vegetable stock
50ml (2fl oz) dry white wine (or extra stock)
1 x 5ml sp (1tsp) chopped fresh parsley
1 x 5ml sp (1tsp) freshly grated vegetarian Parmesan or Pecorino cheese

1. Put the dried mushrooms in a bowl, cover with water; and allow to soak for 30 minutes (see COOK'S TIPS).
2. About 5 minutes before the soaking time is up, heat the oil and butter in a large, lidded, non-stick frying pan and sauté the onion and garlic over a medium heat for about 5 minutes or until soft. Add the fresh mushrooms and black pepper, stir well and cook for 1–2 minutes.
3. Add the rice and soaked mushrooms with their soaking water, stock and wine (if using) and stir. Cover and simmer for 20 minutes, adding a little extra stock or water if it looks dry. Add the courgettes and continue to simmer for a further 10 minutes.
4. When the rice is tender and creamy, stir in the parsley and Parmesan cheese. Serve the risotto with a mixed salad.

COOK'S TIPS
• *Don't use flat field mushrooms as their juices will make the dish go black.*
• *This is an alternative and quick method to cook risotto.*

NUTRITION INFORMATION
per serving

calories	fat	sat fat	salt
435	11.4g	4.5g	0.7g

Vegetable korma with cardamom-scented rice

V | **prep** 10 minutes | **cook** 35–40 minutes | **serves** 1

1 x 5ml sp (1tsp) vegetable oil
1 small onion, peeled and thinly sliced
1 small clove garlic, peeled and crushed
1 x 1.5ml sp (¼tsp) ground cumin
1 x 1.5ml sp (¼tsp) ground coriander
1 x 1.5ml sp (¼tsp) turmeric
1 x 1.5ml sp (¼tsp) garam masala
generous pinch of ground ginger
1 small potato, diced into bite-sized pieces and parboiled
   for 5 minutes
½ small aubergine, cut into 1-cm (½-inch) slices and quartered
25g (1oz) French beans, topped, tailed and halved
150–200ml (5–7fl oz) vegetable stock

50g (1¾oz) basmati rice
150ml (¼pint) water
2 green cardamom pods, lightly crushed

1 x 5ml sp (1tsp) ground almonds
100ml (3½fl oz) 0% fat Greek style yoghurt

1. First prepare the korma. Heat the oil in a non-stick frying pan and stir-fry the onion on medium-high until soft (about 3–4 minutes). Add the garlic and spices and stir for 1 minute.
2. Add the potato, aubergine, beans and half the stock, stir well and bring to simmer. Reduce the heat and simmer for 20 minutes, adding more stock if the mixture looks too dry.
3. Meanwhile, rinse the rice in cold water and put in a small, lidded saucepan, along with the cardamom pods. Cover with water, bring to the boil, reduce the heat, cover and cook for 15 minutes or until tender.
4. Add the ground almonds for the last 2 minutes of cooking the korma.
5. When the vegetables are cooked, add the yoghurt and stir well. Heat for 1–2 minutes (but don't boil). Remove the cardamom pods and serve the korma on a bed of rice.

NUTRITION INFORMATION

per serving

calories	fat	sat fat	salt
430	9g	1.6g	1.5g

Sweet potato curry with lentils

(V) | **prep** 5–7 minutes | **cook** 40 minutes | **serves** 1

1 x 5ml sp (1tsp) vegetable oil
100g (3½oz), peeled weight, sweet potato, cut into bite-sized cubes
75g (2¾oz), peeled weight, potato, cut into bite-sized cubes
1 small onion, peeled and finely chopped
1 small clove garlic, peeled and finely chopped
1 small green chilli, deseeded and chopped
1 x 2.5ml sp (½tsp) ground ginger
50g (1¾ oz) uncooked green lentils
75–100ml (2½–3½fl oz) hot vegetable stock
freshly ground black pepper, to taste
1 x 2.5ml sp (½tsp) garam masala
75–100ml (2½–3½fl oz) hot water
1 x 15ml sp (1tbsp) low-fat natural bio-yoghurt

1. Heat the oil in a non-stick lidded pan and sauté the sweet potato over a medium heat, turning occasionally, for 5 minutes.
2. Meanwhile, bring the potato to the boil, then simmer until almost cooked (about 6 minutes), drain and set aside.
3. When the sweet potato cubes are sautéed, remove them with a slotted spoon and add in the onion. Cook, stirring occasionally, for 5 minutes, or until transparent. Add the garlic, chilli and ginger and stir for 1 minute.
4. Return the sweet potato to the pan with the boiled potato and the lentils, half the stock, seasoning and garam masala, stir well to combine and bring to simmer and cover. Reduce the heat and simmer for 20 minutes, adding a little more water if the curry looks too dry.
5. Stir in the yoghurt and serve with basmati rice.

COOK'S TIPS

• *Scratch the skin of the sweet potato to make sure it is orange-fleshed – the white-fleshed variety is not so good in this recipe.*
• *You could replace sweet potato with pumpkin or butternut squash.*

NUTRITION INFORMATION

per serving

calories	fat	sat fat	salt
315	4.9g	0.9g	0.4g

Tofu and vegetable stir-fry with rice noodles

V | prep 15 minutes + 2 hours marinating | cook 10 minutes | serves 1

100g (3½oz) firm tofu, sliced into strips (see COOK'S TIP)

for the marinade
1 x 5ml sp (1tsp) soy sauce
1 x 15ml sp (1tbsp) lime juice
1 x 5ml sp (1tsp) chopped garlic
1 x 5ml sp (1tsp) chopped lemon grass
1 x 5ml sp (1tsp) chopped root ginger
1 x 5ml sp (1tsp) chopped red chilli

1 x 5ml sp (1tsp) vegetable oil
50g (1¾oz) pak choi, roughly chopped
50g (1¾oz) broccoli florets, roughly chopped
1 small carrot, peeled and cut into thin strips
25g (1oz) beansprouts
1 x 5ml sp (1tsp) vegetarian Thai green curry paste
2 x 15ml sp (2tbsp) vegetable stock
2 spring onions, trimmed and halved lengthways

50g (1¾oz) rice noodles, to serve

1. Put the tofu in a shallow dish. Whisk together the soy sauce and lime juice and pour over the tofu with the other marinade ingredients. If possible, leave to marinate for at least 2 hours (see COOK'S TIP).
2. Cook the noodles according to the packet instructions. Drain and keep warm.
3. Heat the oil in a non-stick wok or large frying pan. Remove the tofu from the marinade, reserving the marinade, and stir-fry the tofu for 1 minute. Add the pak choi, broccoli, carrots and beansprouts and cook, stirring, for a further 1 minute.
4. In a small bowl or cup mix the curry paste, stock and reserved marinade. Add half to the stir-fry mixture and cook for another 2 minutes.
5. Add the remaining paste and marinade mix and the spring onion to the stir-fry and cook for 1 minute, or until the vegetables are just tender. Serve on a bed of warm noodles.

COOK'S TIPS
• *Drain the tofu, wash under a running tap and remove excess water with kitchen paper.*
• *Make time to marinate the tofu as it is quite bland but takes up other flavours well.*

NUTRITION INFORMATION
per serving
(not including the vegetarian Thai green curry paste)

calories	fat	sat fat	salt
360	9.4g	1.3g	1.2g

Vegetable accompaniments and side dishes provide the perfect opportunity to boost both the amount and variety of vegetables in your diet. Although many people automatically assume that fresh

Vegetables and

is best, frozen and canned vegetables also have much to offer. Frozen vegetables are processed within hours of being harvested so their vitamin content is preserved. Studies show that in some cases frozen vegetables actually contain more vitamins than 'fresh' vegetables that may well be a few days old by the time we use them. The vitamins in vegetables are easily lost during storage, preparation and cooking – to maximise your vitamin content the golden rule is to buy the freshest produce available, store in the fridge and eat as soon as possible after purchase. Once cut, the vitamin C will react with the oxygen in the air and be lost, so it's important not to prepare vegetables too far in advance of cooking and eating.

side dishes

Potatoes à la boulangère

 | prep 15 minutes | cook 1 hour | serves 2

400g (14oz), peeled weight, potatoes, very thinly sliced
1 small onion, thinly sliced
freshly ground black pepper, to taste
75ml (2½fl oz) vegetable stock (see COOK'S TIP)
75ml (2½fl oz) skimmed milk
1 x 5ml sp (1tsp) butter

1. Preheat the oven to 180°C/350°F/Gas Mark 4.
2. Layer the potato and onion slices in a shallow, ovenproof dish, seasoning each layer well.
3. Mix the milk and stock and pour over the potatoes. Dot the top layer with the butter, cover with foil and bake in the oven for 30 minutes.
4. Remove the foil and continue to cook for a further 30 minutes or until the potatoes are cooked.

COOK'S TIPS
• *You can use an alternative to the onion such as leeks or mixed peppers.*
• *You could use chicken stock instead of vegetable stock if catering for non-vegetarians.*

NUTRITION INFORMATION

per serving

calories	fat	sat fat	salt
200	2.8g	1.5g	0.5g

Spinach and butternut squash bake

V | **prep** 20 minutes | **cook** 40 minutes | **serves** 2

for the baked vegetables
250g (9oz) peeled weight, butternut squash, deseeded and cut into
   bite-sized cubes
2 small red onions, each cut into 8 segments
2 x 5ml sp (2tsp) light vegetable or olive oil
freshly ground black pepper, to taste

for the white sauce
250ml (9fl oz) skimmed milk
20g (¾oz) cornflour
1 x 5ml sp (1tsp) mustard powder
2 small bay leaves
1 small onion
4 x 5ml sp (4tsp) freshly grated vegetarian Parmesan or Pecorino cheese
120g (4¼oz) baby spinach leaves

for the topping
2 x 15ml sp (2tbsp) wholemeal breadcrumbs

1. Preheat the oven to 200°C/400°F/Gas Mark 6 and warm an ovenproof serving dish.
2. Arrange the prepared squash and onion on a non-stick baking tray and coat with the oil and plenty of black pepper. Bake for 20 minutes, turning once.
3. To make the sauce, put the milk into a small non-stick saucepan with the flour, mustard, onion and bay leaf. Whisk over a medium heat until thick. Remove from the heat, discard the onion and bay leaf and stir in the cheese. Set aside, stirring occasionally, to prevent a skin forming.
4. When the squash is nearly cooked, put the spinach in a large saucepan with 1 tablespoon of water, stirring, for 2–3 minutes or until just wilted.
5. You can continue cooking this dish in the hot oven, or preheat the grill to medium-high. Put half the squash mixture in the warmed ovenproof dish and top with half the spinach. Repeat the layers. Pour over the white sauce and sprinkle over the breadcrumbs.
6. Either put under the preheated grill until browned and bubbling, or transfer to the oven for 15–20 minutes.

COOK'S TIP
• *Lightly boiled, steamed or microwaved cauliflower florets can be added to the squash for extra bulk.*

NUTRITION INFORMATION

per serving

calories	fat	sat fat	salt
120	3.9g	1.4g	0.4g

Sweet and sour red cabbage

(V) | prep 5 minutes | cook 45–55 minutes | serves 2

200g (7oz) red cabbage, prepared weight, any tough core removed, finely sliced
1 medium cooking apple, peeled, cored and chopped
1 shallot, finely chopped
1 x 15ml sp (1tbsp) wine vinegar, red or white
1 x 15ml sp (1tbsp) brown sugar
1 x 5ml sp (1tsp) butter
freshly ground black pepper, to taste

1. Put all the ingredients in a heavy-based, lidded saucepan or flame-proof casserole with 2 x 15ml sp (2tbsp) water. Season to taste.
2. Cook over a medium-low heat for 15 minutes, stir well and replace lid. Reduce the heat and simmer for 30–40 minutes, stirring once or twice.
3. When the cabbage is tender, check the seasoning and serve.

COOK'S TIP
• *This dish can also be cooked in the oven, 170°C/325°F/Gas Mark 3, for the same amount of time.*

NUTRITION INFORMATION

per serving

calories	fat	sat fat	salt
105	2.5g	1.4g	trace

Courgettes with mustard seeds

 | prep 5 minutes | cook 10–15 minutes | serves 2

1 x 5ml sp (1tsp) vegetable or
   olive oil
1 clove garlic, peeled and crushed
1 x 2.5ml sp (½tsp) black mustard
   seeds
1 x 2.5ml sp (½tsp) ground cumin
1 x 2.5ml sp (½tsp) coriander seeds
½ red chilli, deseeded and
   finely chopped
2 medium courgettes, trimmed
   and sliced
200g (7oz) canned tomatoes, chopped
1 x 15ml sp (1tbsp) chopped fresh
   coriander leaves or parsley

1. Heat the oil in a non-stick lidded pan.
Add the garlic, dry spices and chilli, stir
over a medium heat and then remove
for 2 minutes.
2. Add the courgettes and tomatoes and
cook for about 5–10 minutes or until
tender, adding a tablespoon of water if
necessary. Stir in the fresh coriander or
parsley and serve.

COOK'S TIP
• *As a change from courgettes, try okra or
serve the sauce over French beans.*

Glazed parsnips with sesame seeds

 | prep 5 minutes | cook 20 minutes | serves 2

2 parsnips, peeled and cut into
   even-sized chunks
1 x 5ml sp (1tsp) runny honey
1 x 2.5ml sp (½tsp) sesame seeds

1. Preheat the oven to 200°C/400°F/
Gas Mark 7.
2. Put the parsnips in a pan of water,
bring to the boil and cook for 5 minutes.
Drain well.
3. Transfer the parsnips to a roasting tin,
brush with honey and roast in the oven for
10 minutes.
4. Sprinkle over the sesame seeds and
cook for a further 5 minutes.

COOK'S TIP
• *You can prepare carrots in the same way.*

*Opposite fore-
ground: Glazed
parsnips with
sesame seeds;
background:
Courgettes with
mustard seeds*

NUTRITION INFORMATION

per serving

calories	fat	sat fat	salt
60	2.5g	0.5g	0.1g

NUTRITION INFORMATION

per serving

calories	fat	sat fat	salt
100	2.0g	0.4g	trace

You don't have to miss out on dessert just because you're on a diet. Puddings don't have to be high in fat and sugar. Fresh fruit or a fruit salad is an excellent way to finish a meal and will help you reach the recommended target of 5 daily

Desserts

servings of fruit and/or vegetables. But if you fancy something a little more decadent there are plenty of low-fat options available. Presentation plays an important role in our enjoyment of food and can transform a simple dessert into a special one. A sprig of fresh mint, a light dusting of icing sugar or a slice of fresh fruit as a garnish can make a real difference.

0.5% FAT   **135** CALORIES

Meringues with lime cream and raspberries

V | **prep** 5 minutes | **serves** 1

2½ x 15ml sp (2½tbsp) natural bio-yoghurt (less than 2% fat)
2 x 5ml sp (2tsp) icing sugar
grated zest and juice of ¼ lime
1 meringue nest
25g (1oz) raspberries

1. Mix the yoghurt, icing sugar, lime zest and juice.
2. Place a meringue nest on a plate, pour in the yoghurt mixture, sprinkle with raspberries and serve.

COOK'S TIP
• *You can substitute frozen fruits of the forest for the raspberries or use fresh fruit in season.*

NUTRITION INFORMATION

per serving

calories	fat	sat fat	salt
135	0.5g	0.3g	0.2g

0.1% FAT
130 CALORIES

Strawberry and orange jelly

prep 10 minutes + 30 minutes cooling │ **cook** 5 minutes │ **serves** 2

400ml (14fl oz) orange juice (see COOK'S TIP)
1 x 15ml sp (1tbsp) gelatine, or vegetarian equivalent
90g (3¼oz) small strawberries, sliced

1. Put 100ml (3½fl oz) of the juice in a small heatproof bowl, sprinkle over the gelatine and leave to stand for 5 minutes. Place the bowl over a pan of simmering water and stir until the gelatine melts and the liquid becomes clear, then stir in the remaining juice.
2. Divide the strawberries between 2 large wine glasses. Pour over enough juice to just cover the strawberries and transfer to the fridge for 30 minutes or until set.
3. Pour in the remaining juice and return to the fridge until set.

COOK'S TIPS
• When strawberries are out of season use seedless grapes instead.
• You could use another juice instead of orange, such as passion fruit (but not pineapple).

NUTRITION INFORMATION

per serving

calories	fat	sat fat	salt
130	0.2g	trace	0.2g

Spiced pineapple with mango sauce

(V) | **prep** 10 minutes | **cook** 5 minutes | **serves** 2

for the sauce
1 small ripe mango, peeled and stone removed
125ml (4fl oz) orange juice
1 x 5ml sp (1tsp) arrowroot
1 x 2.5ml sp (½tsp) mixed spice
1 x 5ml sp (1tsp) melted butter
2 x 5ml sp (2tsp) demerara sugar

2 thick slices fresh pineapple

1. First make the sauce. Put the mango and orange juice in a blender and purée until smooth. Tip the purée into a small pan. Mix the arrowroot with a little cold water and add to the pan. Heat gently, stirring constantly, until the sauce begins to thicken.
2. Preheat the grill. Stir the mixed spice into the melted butter. Place the pineapple on a foil-covered baking tray. Brush the pineapple with the melted butter, sprinkle over the sugar and put under a medium-hot grill for 5 minutes.
3. Transfer the pineapple to a plate, pour over a little of the sauce and serve warm (see COOK'S TIP).

COOK'S TIP
• *Decorate with delicate physalis (Cape gooseberries) for that added touch.*

NUTRITION INFORMATION

per serving

calories	fat	sat fat	salt
145	2.4g	1.4g	trace

Roasted peach with vanilla sugar

V | **prep** 10 minutes | **cook** 15–20 minutes | **serves** 1

for the vanilla sugar
25g (1oz) caster sugar
¼ vanilla pod

1 small ripe peach, halved and stoned
2 x 15ml sp (2tbsp) low-fat natural yoghurt

1. Preheat the oven to 200°C/400°F/Gas Mark 6.
2. Scrape out the sticky seeds from the vanilla pod and blend with the sugar in an electric hand blender.
3. Place the peach, flesh-side up, in an ovenproof dish and sprinkle over the vanilla sugar.
4. Bake for 15–20 minutes, or until tender, and serve with natural yoghurt.

COOK'S TIPS
• *If your peach is under-ripe, allow 20–30 minutes cooking time.*
• *This dish also works well with nectarines and plums – allow 1 nectarine or 2 plums per serving.*
• *A batch of vanilla sugar can be made ahead and kept for several weeks in a jar.*

NUTRITION INFORMATION
per serving

calories	fat	sat fat	salt
140	0.2g	0.2g	trace

Apple and sultana filo parcels with vanilla yoghurt

(V) | **prep** 5 minutes | **cook** 20–25 minutes | **serves** 2

for filo parcels (makes 2)
1 medium Bramley apple, peeled, cored and cut into small chunks
15g (½oz) sultanas
2 x 5ml sp (2tsp) sugar
1 x 5ml sp (1tsp) lemon juice
pinch of ground cinnamon
6 sheets filo pastry, approximately 22 x 28mm (¾ x 1¼inches)
1 egg white, beaten
1 x 15ml sp (1tbsp) skimmed milk

for vanilla yoghurt
few drops of vanilla essence
100ml (3½fl oz) low-fat natural bio-yoghurt, to serve

  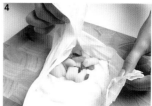

1. Preheat the oven to 200°C/400°F/Gas Mark 6.
2. Put the apples in a small saucepan with 2 x 5ml sp (2tsp) of water. Simmer over a gentle heat for a few minutes or until the apples are just soft. Take care not to overcook the apples as they will continue cooking in the oven.
3. Drain any excess liquid from the apples then stir in the sultanas, sugar, lemon juice and cinnamon.
4. Take 3 sheets of filo, one on top of the other, and brush with the egg white. Spoon the apple mixture into the centre and gather up the pastry edges to form a bag around the filling. Pinch the pastry together with your fingers to seal it. Repeat with the remaining 3 sheets. Work quickly with the filo pastry as it goes dry quickly.
5. Place the parcels on a baking tray and brush with the milk.
6. Bake for 20–25 minutes or until golden brown. Allow to cool for a few minutes.
7. Stir the vanilla essence into the yoghurt and serve with the filo parcels.

NUTRITION INFORMATION

per serving (1 filo parcel)

calories	fat	sat fat	salt
150	1.1g	0.3g	0.1g

Baked banana with sin-free chocolate sauce

Ⓥ | **prep** 1 minute | **cook** 10 minutes | **serves** 1

1 small banana
2 x 5ml sp (2tsp) golden syrup
3 x 5ml sp (3tsp) cocoa powder

1. Preheat the oven to 180C°/350°F/Gas Mark 4.
2. Bake the banana in its skin for 10 minutes, or until the skin is black.
3. Meanwhile, warm the syrup in a small saucepan over a medium heat for 2–3 minutes, or in a medium-low microwave for 1 minute until very runny. Stir in the cocoa powder until smooth and chocolate-like. Keep warm.
4. When the banana is cooked, discard the skin, put the flesh on a plate, pour the chocolate sauce over and serve.

COOK'S TIP
• *You could, alternatively, bake your bananas on the barbecue until their skins turn black.*

NUTRITION INFORMATION
per serving

calories	fat	sat fat	salt
140	2.6g	0.6g	0.2g

Chocolate and orange liqueur mousse

prep 5 minutes + 40 minutes soaking | **serves** 1

Opposite left: Chocolate and orange liqueur mousse; right: Rum and raisin chocolate mousse

1 x 2.5ml sp (½tsp) grated orange zest
1 x 5ml sp (1tsp) Cointreau
1 count on us... chocolate mousse, 70g (2½oz)
1 meringue nest, lightly crushed

1. Put the zest in an eggcup with the Cointreau and soak for at least 30 minutes.
2. Empty the chocolate mousse into a bowl and stir in the meringue. Spoon into a sundae dish (see COOK'S TIP).
3. Refrigerate for at least 10 minutes, and serve, with the orange zest and Cointreau spooned over.

COOK'S TIP

• *For an attractive layered effect (as shown opposite), spoon half of the chocolate mousse into a sundae dish, followed by the meringue, followed by the rest of the mousse.*

Rum and raisin chocolate mousse

prep 10 minutes + 30 minutes soaking | **serves** 1

1 x 5ml sp (1tsp) raisins
1 x 15ml sp (1tbsp) dark rum
1 amaretto biscuit (optional)
1 count on us... chocolate mousse, 70g (2½oz)

1. Put the raisins in a teacup, pour over the rum and allow to stand for at least 30 minutes, preferably overnight.
2. Stir the rum, raisins and amaretto biscuit into the chocolate mousse. Spoon into a sundae dish and serve.

COOK'S TIP

• *Amaretti biscuits are a useful ingredient for slimming desserts because they are very light and are only 8% fat, but use them sparingly as they are high in sugar.*

NUTRITION INFORMATION
per serving

calories	fat	sat fat	salt
140	1.9g	trace	trace

NUTRITION INFORMATION
per serving

calories	fat	sat fat	salt
150	2.3g	1.2g	trace

3% FAT **150** CALORIES

Pear and chocolate cream

prep 5 minutes | can be made ahead and chilled | **serves** 1

75g (2¾oz) canned pears in juice (drained weight)
75g (2¾oz) virtually fat-free fromage frais (see COOK'S TIP)
few drops of vanilla essence
15g (½oz) milk chocolate, grated

1. Purée the pears in an electric blender, or mash thoroughly with a fork.
2. In a mixing bowl, combine the pears, fromage frais and vanilla essence, then lightly stir in two-thirds of the chocolate.
3. Spoon into a single-serving dessert glass or dish and top with the remaining chocolate. Chill before serving.

COOK'S TIP
• *Instead of adding vanilla essence to fromage frais, you can buy vanilla-flavoured fromage frais.*

NUTRITION INFORMATION

per serving

calories	fat	sat fat	salt
150	4.7g	2.7g	0.1g

Index